Copywriting For Beginners Guide:

The Ultimate Copywriter's Handbook to Writing Powerful Advertising, Sales and Marketing Copy

By

Robert Alderman

ISBN-13: 978-1508527671

Table of Contents

Copywriting For Beginners Guide: The Ultimate Copywriter's Handbook to Writing Powerful Advertising, Sales and Marketing Copy

By Robert Alderman

This publication is designed to provide accurate and authoritative information in regard to the subject matter covered. This work is sold with the understanding that the publisher is not engaged in rendering legal, accounting, or other professional services. If legal advice or other expert assistance is required, the services of a competent professional person should be sought.

First Published, 2015

Printed in the United States of America

Introduction

Copywriting refers to a copy written for advertising and publicity purposes and aims to convince or compel the target audience. Copywriting services are offered by marketing and advertising agencies and utilized by commercial organizations to promote their ideas, brand, product or services. The purpose of copywriting is to get across a message in such an effective way that it not only reaches to its target audience but helps shape a favorable opinion as well and eventually leads to a desirable action.

Copywriting is a creative piece of writing which does not merely involves the features and benefits of a product with intimate details but also focuses on what your target audience needs and wants, ties them up emotionally, make them think this is exactly what they want and convince them to buy a product or brand.

Chapter 1. Rules of Copywriting

Copywriting is an expert job which requires a great understanding of how to convey a marketing message in a compelling and meaningful manner and how to positively engage your target audience. In order to achieve this purpose, an expert copywriter is needed. A marketing message written by someone who is not an expert may cause damage to the overall objective and may put your entire marketing campaign at a risk of falling.

However, there are some general rules involved in copywriting and without these rules desired results cannot be achieved.

- The marketing message has to be written from the perspective of your potential customers and it should be about their needs and requirements, not merely what you want to tell them about your product or service. If your marketing message does not sound like that, replace it altogether or make changes in it until it becomes something valuable for your audience.

- Copywriting is of no value if message is not conveyed the way it supposed to be. The marketing message has to communicate with the target audience properly and in an easily understandable manner. It should tell them clearly what is in for them or what are the benefits they are going to get when they buy a certain product or service. If the potential costumer is unable to understand the message how he is expected to take the appropriate or indented action.

- Keep your message simple. Avoid using big, completed and irrelevant words. Sometimes you like a word or have a word in your mind and you just want to put it in your marketing message. Words that are not relevant to your message or idea can reduce the impact of the message and can cause damage to your overall advertising campaign.

- The most important thing while crafting copywriting is the selection of words. Whatever word is chosen, it has to hold a meaning and must go with the overall flow of the message. Avoid using words that may cause distraction from the actual idea and put your target audience in a state of confusion. Improper choice of words may waste your whole effort and money.

- Do not claim anything you are not offering to your target audience. Although, any such claims will immediately uplift your sales but eventually lead to a slump when customer will not find the benefits they were promised. Just explain them clearly what they are likely to expect in a product, brand or service. It will help make your marketing message more compelling and captivating. However, you need to add emotional angles to entice your target audience and make them act desirably.

- It is widely believed that almost 80 percent of the copy should base around "you" rather than "I" or "We". It means your copy should provide the answers to the questions arising in the mind of the customers. A copywriter must have an ability to create a right kind of balance between the needs of the company and the needs of the customers and this is what exactly matters when it comes to constructing an effective marketing message.

- The copy has to precise and to the point. Do not clutter it with too many words and information. The ideal copy has to be something easy to digest for the target audience, not something that will go straight over their head, leaving an ambiguous and vague impression.

Chapter 2. How to Write an Effective Copy?

Copywriting is an art of successfully marketing your product, idea or service. Writing a successful or an effective copy is not like pulling off the magic, it demands a lot of creativity and focus on minor details. The ultimate purpose of the copy is to persuade target audience and sell your product, service or brand.

The following is a step by step description of an effective copywriting.

Get an idea about the product or service

Firstly, it is important to get a clear about the product, brand or service you are going to write about. Generally, you need to know what is the brand or the product, the name of the company that has launched it and the general traits and qualities of the product. These are the basics of copywriting, without knowing them you cannot even start off writing.

Determine the "USP" of the product

USP is the acronym of "Unique Selling Proposition" which includes all those factors that are unique and make a product different from its competitors. For instance, your product has low rates in comparison to the competitors or it is more durable than your competitor's product. You will get all these information when you research the products of your competitors as well. What are the features of their products and what incentives they are offering to their customers? When you compare your product from your competitors only then you will come to know the USP of your product and highlight it in your copy.

Understand your target audience

The target audience is the group the product or service is aimed at. Knowing about your target audience is very important for crafting an effective marketing message. You cannot frame your message correctly if you are not clearly understood your target audience, their mindset, their preferences, their needs and requirements. So you need to take a lot of time to research your potential customers. In case the product is launched at limited scale and the allotted budget is also very low, do not make your research too complex. Generally, you need to know the gender, age group and the social status of the target audience.

The medium of the marketing message

Medium of the marketing message is another important thing you need know prior to writing a copy. Each medium requires specific tone and writing style and you need to adjust your copy keeping in mind that medium. For instance, an ad message placed on the billboard requires few captivating words or a crisp headline to grab the attention of the potential buyers whereas a marketing message published in a magazine will provide you more space and time to convince your reader. The tone will be changed from one medium to another in order to make it more compelling and captivating.

Layout of the page

The graphics, font size, the placement of the marketing message and the overall layout also have an effect on the voice of your message. These factors may not directly affect the sales of a product or brand but certainly they will help bring the attention towards your sales message. A copywriter must need to know the make-up of the page before drafting an advertising message.

Catchy and relevant headline

A catchy headline is very important to bring your potential customer in to view an advertising message. A catchy headline is something which let a reader stop and entice him to read the full message. But the headline has to be relevant with the product and the message written on it. It will create a bad impression if a headline is attractive yet it has nothing to do with the advertising message. Try to make a balance out of attractiveness and factuality.

Use conversational tone

Conversational style of writing is considered quite successful to reach to your target audience and to make them think about your product or service. But your approach has to be sophisticated and within the boundaries of decency. Also, avoid using those words which make your message look like controversial and confusing. The message has to be written in such a way that it is addressed to a single person of a specific group but communicates with the group as whole.

Avoid too much information

Being concise and compact is better rather than stuffing it with too much information. Do not include the information that can be important but may cause to imbalance your message and make it sound less effective. Add only that information that is most relevant and most important for your target audience. Too many details may cloud their mind and make them forget the aspects that you really want them to remember. Write you copy in an interesting yet simplified manner.

Do not use filler words

Avoid using filler words in your copywriting. It is a big no no when it comes to writing an effective marketing message. The filler words can be very, quite, really or any other word of such sort. These words will do nothing except cluttering your copy and making it more heavy and lengthy. Sometimes, the inclusion of these words may sound your message too casual and relaxed and this is not the tone you want for your message.

More focus on benefits rather than features

Talk about the benefits of the product more rather than the features. The feature and benefits might be taken as the same but there is a huge difference between them. A feature explains the product itself and its function while benefits describe what the product will do for its buyer. A good mix of features and benefits can lead to an even more desirable result. For instance, this sentence "the rich creamy lather of the soap will give your skin a smooth and soft texture" can be easily used for the marketing of a soap or face wash or a copywriter can add this sentence for creating a marketing message for a sun protection product "it contains SPF 10 which protects your skin from ultraviolet rays of the sun". Both above mentioned sentences signify the feature of the product as well as its benefits for the users.

Emotional appeal

The marketing message is aimed towards human beings not for the robots. If emotional words are used in copywriting, they can have certain kind of appeal for the customers and can increase the conversion rate. According to many marketing experts there are seven key drivers or emotional hot buttons to use in copywriting: fear, greed, guilt, anger, exclusivity, salvation and flattery. If a copywriting is not able to trigger one of these, the copy is useless and has to be written all over again.

Make your copy sound more clear and understandable

Avoid using words and sentences which may confuse your customers. Replace them with more clear and alive words and sentences. For instance, if you are writing a copy about a person who is in the field of event manager, you can write "he is the finest event manager in the country". But you can make this sentence more clear and compelling if it is structured in such way "he organizes corporate events better than anyone else right now". Do not become too much predictable and boring. Add new and fresh perspective and play around with words and ideas. Write a sentence over and over again until you feel that this the best possible way I can structure my sentence.

Create fascination

As it is mentioned above, do not become too much predictable when it comes to copywriting. Do not follow the same pattern used by your competitors or the professional ahead of you. Think out of the box and put forward new dimensions and perspectives in front of your viewers or readers. Do not try to persuade people with the same old ideas and tricks which have been repeated over and over again in the past. If you have a new idea in your mind and you think it suits your product as well, make it a part of your marketing message.

Compelling enough to make customers continue reading

Your copy has to be compelling enough to make the reader stay and continue reading. Ideally, a marketing message should force them to stop, have a glance on it, convince them to take an action and to purchase a product or service. If reader or listener does not look further and leave the page immediately after having a glance, how can you expect to complete the rest of the process? Your copy should hold interest right from the beginning. Try to add some twists, a question, a fact or anything else which can help grab the attention right from the start. If readers or viewers found it plain and dull, they are unlikely to stick to your copy.

Construction of the sentences

Construct your sentences properly. Proper construction does not necessarily mean to follow the rules of grammar and punctuation but each sentence has to flow nicely and look a part of the paragraph. It should not appear that you have forcibly added a sentence to just fill the gap. Breaking the grammatical rules is allowed as far as your copy flows nicely and reads well. If you feel any sentence is looking odd and does not seems to be a part of the message, remove it immediately from the copy. Replace it with an altogether new sentence or make changes in the sentence to make it look appropriate.

Proofread your work

Once you think your copy is done and is ready to submit to the respective organization, review it again in order to proofread your work. Delete all those sentences and words which look unnecessary or misfit upon review. Continue trimming until length is shortened and the copy looks organized, compact and up to the mark. The final draft can also be send to the commercial organization to get their view as well. If they are satisfied with the outcome, they will accept it as it is. If they need any changes, they will send it back to you for modification.

Chapter 3. Qualities of a Copywriter

Copywriter is the professional responsible for crafting a marketing and sales message. Like any other professional, certain kind of requisites are required for successful copywriting.

Quick learner

A copywriter must have a curious nature and must have an ability to learn new things quickly. If he starts thinking that his knowledge his impeccable and he does not require any improvement, the quality of his work will suffer and start to decrease as well.

Creative

Creativity is probably the most important skill a copywriter is expected to have. Obviously, a copywriter is going to be briefed about every assigned project but at the same time he is also expected to incorporate his own innovative thinking into the basic theme and to introduce new dimensions and perspectives. The combination of both, following the instructions and adding own creativity is necessary for crafting an effective marketing message.

Good at research

A copywriter has to be someone not afraid of rigorous research. Research is the only way a copywriter can learn about his target audience, their thinking, their needs and requirements and their attitude. Research is also necessary to learn about the competitors and for knowing their strength and weaknesses and strategies. With thorough research, a copywriter can differentiate his product and the products of the competitors, exploit their strength and weaknesses and capitalize on their mistakes.

Brainstorm ideas

Sometimes the copywriter is not provided with the basic theme. It is because the organization has nothing new to work on and they are in search of new themes and ideas. In such cases, copywriter is expected to use his imagination and brainstorm new ideas and fresh perspectives. But the idea has to be applicable and offers something new and interesting and has to fascinating for your readers, listeners or viewers.

Command over the language

A copywriter must have a firm grip on the language on which he writes his marketing messages. If a copywriter does not possess a command over language, his message will lack the kind of affect which is expected to be in the message. The basics of the language have to be spot on. The flaws and mistakes in the grammar make your marketing message look ugly and improper.

Know the elements of copywriting

Knowing the basics of copywriting is absolute necessary for a copywriter. The copywriting is comprised of several elements such as headline, taglines and captions. Knowing these elements and more importantly how to use them properly is necessary for crafting an effective copy.

Take criticism constructively

A copywriter is someone who takes criticism constructively and utilizes it to improve his own work. A criticism is a thing which can be painful and demoralizing but a copywriter must have an ability to accept it gracefully. The reaction should not be arguing or defending your work instead he should try to find out where the mistake lies and what steps can be taken to improve the work and to take it up to the desired standard.

Detail oriented

Being detail oriented is quality a copywriter expected to have. Like many other professions, it is a way to excel and advance in the field of copywriting as well. Paying attention to both major and minor details is critical in creating a compelling copy. If a copywriter has a tendency to ignore details, his work will suffer immensely. His final copy will be send back again and again for corrections and to improve your work.

Use of emotions

A copywriter must know how to use and trigger human emotions. If copywriter is not able to touch his target audience emotionally or involve them emotionally into a product or service, the marketing message is of no value and it will not be able to create desired results.

Chapter 4. Elements of Copywriting

The marketing and sales messages are important tools for the success of a business. It is necessary to understand how the elements of copywriting or sales messages work together and support the overall marketing campaign.

There are two basic purposes of a successful copywriting. First to build a relationship with the target audience, attach them emotionally with the product and make them think that product is of great value to them. Second is to convince them to act and purchase a product or hire the services. A successful copy manages to produce a significant amount of effect on the buying decisions of the people.

Kicker

Kicker is a line which grabs the attention of the reader and compels them to read the headline or even the entire message.

Headline

Headline is undoubtedly the most important element of the copywriting. It is the headline that sets the tone for the remainder of the copy and can make or break the whole marketing campaign. If headline is written in an impressive and interesting way, it will urge the reader to continue reading and have a look at entire message. But an unimpressive and poorly written headline may push your potential customers away and eventually affects your sales.

The headline has to be short, crisp and captivating. It must have something unique and informative to share. It should not read the same as the thousands of other headlines in other advertising copies time and again. In copywriting, headline is the prime focus of the copywriter. Usually, a copywriter has to write multiple headlines before few are selected for the marketing message and even fewer are actually used in the message.

Subheadings

Subheadings, as the name suggests are placed underneath the headline. The subheads are usually included in a copy to arouse the interest of the reader and to carry it into the body of the message.

Body copy

Body copy contains the benefits and features of the products or service. This part of the copywriting should be written in a simple yet interesting way so the potential customers have a clear idea about the product, its function and more importantly they should know what benefits they are going to get after purchasing it.

The main purposes of the body copy are introducing the product to the customers and help them remember the name and its benefits. The body copy is the copywriting element that takes most of the time and it is said that many of the best copywriters spend weeks just creating the headline and may take months to write the body copy. This is because they know how important the body copy is for crafting effective marking message so they take their time to get it right and up to the standard.

Body copy demands a lot of creativity on the part of a copywriter. It can be constructed either in the form of paragraphs or benefits and features can be listed in the bullets. No matter whatever form is chosen, it should promise to solve one or few of the problems of the customers.

Body copy can vary in length depending on the nature of the product but generally it is believed that a brief and concise copy body holds more interest for the readers. Keep it short so it does not sound dull and boring.

Use common and short words. The body copy is meant for the people. Do not try to make it too literary correct. As long as they are making sense and flowing nicely, they are perfect for the readers or viewers. The body copy should touch the audience emotionally. Use emotions in the body copy which stimulates the hot buttons of the audience.

Testimonials

A testimonial is statement provided by satisfied customers to certify the value or excellence of the product. Satisfied customers are those who have already purchased your product, use it and affirm that product possesses the benefits and the features claimed by the company or manufacturers of the product.

Chapter 5. Additional Copywriting Tips

The great copy written for marketing should act a like a salesperson of a company who is working 24/7, trying to convince people to have a look at their product and buy it. Here are some tips for drafting an effective copywriting.

In-depth research is necessary before starting off the writing process. If you are unaware of your target audience, you may pull off something which does not promise to fulfill their actual needs and requirements. A copywriter must know what is important for his target audience. Anything which is distant to reality lacks the appeal for the buyers.

Do not underestimate the people whom you are writing for. They have ability to reason and act accordingly. If they are not satisfied with the way the product and its benefits are explained, they may not be able to take the desired action which is obviously to purchase the respective product or service.

Do not use unnecessary and non meaningful words and sentences just to fill up the space. Keep it informative, readable and useful for the target audience. A copywriter must have a natural flair of writing persuasively without playing too many tricks.

Offer you target audience something new and fresh. Tell them something which they have never seen or heard before. Storytelling is a great way to entice and persuade them.

Do not afraid of taking risks. Try to come up with something unexpected and thrilling. The risk factor more often than not helps you achieve the desired results.

Final Words

Copywriting is a tool that helps promote the overall marketing campaign and the success of a sales and marketing campaign hugely depends on the success of a copywriting. So it is necessary to create a clear, compact and lively writing in order to capture the attention of the potential costumers. The effective copywriting results in the improvement of return on investment (ROI) and boost in the sales.

Thank You Page

I want to personally thank you for reading my book. I hope you found information in this book useful and I would be very grateful if you could leave your honest review about this book. I certainly want to thank you in advance for doing this.

If you have the time, you can check my other books too.